Beautiful

Bipolar

A Book About Bipolar Disorder

By Danielle Workman

Beautiful Bipolar

A Book about Bipolar Disorder

Written by Danielle Workman

Cover Art by Emily Nikolaisen

Printed by Createspace

2017

Printed in the United States of America

First Printing, 2017

ISBN -13 978-1548219581

ISBN - 10 1548219584

http://thisworkmanlife.com

Dedication

To the "crazy ones". The ones who are told that they are insane. The ones who lie awake at night, dreading the sunrise and the return to reality. The ones who are told that they will never be cured. This book is for you.

To my family and dear friends. Thank you for your support, your love, and your kindness. You have literally saved my life and allowed me to write this book. This book exists because of you.

And finally, to my husband and my son. Thank you for being the most amazing people that I have ever met. I'm sorry that momma is a crazy motherfucker, but let's face it, it makes life more interesting.

Thank you. I love you.
This book is for you.

Table of Contents

Preface

"What is it that you like to do outside of just...life?" My therapist asked. He leaned back in his chair and scribbled something down on his little yellow Steno pad. It was a hot June afternoon, the air conditioner sitting above my chair, blowing my hair softly against my cheeks. Despite the cool air blowing on me, I felt as if I could fall asleep in that stuffy office.

The office was oddly comforting, which was ironic because the therapy sessions always made me so uncomfortable. The walls were painted a light mocha color, and the leather couch sitting to my right was once a dark brown, but now faded and worn. I sat in a black leather armchair with arm rests that were way too high and a cushion way too soft. The longer I sat in the chair, the more I sunk into it, feeling small and insecure. I had been sitting in the armchair for forty minutes, facing my therapist who was also sitting in an armchair. He and I had not had much in the way of a meaningful appointment so far, and it wasn't looking like the last few minutes was going to be one.

"Oh," I started to reply, sighing deeply. Shifting uncomfortably in my seat, I leaned back as well and adjusted my shirt. "I, uh, I write." I said cautiously, folding my arms across my chest. "But not like a book or poetry or anything. I write on my website, my blog." My voice trailed off as I stopped, feeling embarrassed. Everyone and their dog had a blog or a website these days, yet no respectable person would dare mention it publicly.

"So you enjoy writing?" My therapist asked.

"Yeah, I do." I said with a nod. "But I write to bring in extra money for my family, it is not really anything I do for pleasure or anything…"

"So you *don't* like writing?" My therapist asked, trying to understand my rambling.

"No," I said quietly. "I love it actually. I just haven't written in years." I paused to collect my thoughts. "Not since I was told I'd never become an author." My voice and my mind trailed off. As I sat in the silence, I was taken back to that fateful evening. My father called me into the family office, where I found he had laid out my notebooks. Some of them lay open and sprawled out across the desk, others lay closed in a pile in the corner of the room. I sat on a folding chair, facing my dad as he gave me his opinion on my writing.

"You're okay," He started, sighing deeply. "But you're never going to be a great author like Anne Rice or J.K. Rowling." My dad suggested I read Anne Rice's novels, and handed me worn out copies of her books. Instead of accepting them and that opinion as a challenge, I saw it as a death sentence for my dreams. I quit writing, ending most of my other creative endeavors as well. A few years later, those notebooks all disappeared without warning, and with it my last glimpses of my childhood dreams.

Blinking, I looked back to my therapist. "It was a childhood dream. I'm not sure it will ever become a reality."

"Well, our time is up, but let's put this on the docket for next week." My therapist replied. He uncrossed his legs and leaned forward. "I have homework for you."

"Hold on," I said, leaning forward and digging deep into my purse. I pulled out my notebook and opened it.

Even though it was brand new, it was tattered and worn, even though it was only a few months old. Pictures and quotes were taped inside of it from magazines and newspapers, making it bulky. The varied colors and thicknesses of the inks used bled onto other pages. I opened it and tried to find an empty page to write on a midst all the clutter of my other notes. "Whoa." He laughed, looking at my notebook. "Looks like that thing has seen some life."

"Yeah," I said smiling, looking down and touching the worn pages. "I actually started writing every little thing down when I decided to go to get treatment for my Bipolar Disorder. Every thought, every medication dose, every side effect, conversations...it's all in here."

"May I see some of it?" He asked. I nodded and flipped through the pages, trying to find a worthwhile entry to share. I finally found one and handed him the notebook. It was an entry about one of our appointments, what he had said and how I felt before and after our meeting. I remember it was a therapy session that I had some serious progress.

"I need to be like a pickle." He began to read out loud. "Instead of dying from the vinegar of life and becoming vile and wrinkly from it, I just need to accept it and transform from a crappy cucumber into a delicious dill pickle." We both laughed out loud. It was not one of my best written entries, but it was one of the many ridiculous analogies about my current journey with getting well.

"Not my best work." I admitted, sheepishly.

"I really think this is great." He said, closing the notebook and handing it back to me. "I don't know who made you believe you cannot be a great author, but they are wrong. If anything you turn into a book or a novel is as good as some of those entries..." He chuckled. "Even the pickle one." I nodded as he spoke.

"Deep down, I want to write a book about all of this." I admitted. "I want to publish a book that isn't all holier-than-thou and that is raw, and honest and…" I paused for a moment as I collected my thoughts. "Everything I've read, everything I've seen, everyone is too scared to talk honestly about the real bullshit we go through." I said loudly, as if I was declaring something. Embarrassed, I put my fingers against my lips.

"Like what?" My therapist asked softly.

"Suicide. Cutting. Medications. Delirium. Psychosis. The drama. The pain… the thought processes…" I sighed loudly and shook my head. "Sorry, I'm rambling."

"Dani." He said, smiling softly at me. "Please write this book. Not just for yourself and not because I would like to read it, but for all those people that deserve that book. The world needs a book like that. Please be the one to write it."

Beautiful Bipolar

To the Beautiful, Bold, Bipolar;

The culture of today is fast paced, moving at a breakneck speed. With the technological savviness of social media sitting in the forefront of most of our minds, our culture has come to not only know but expect perfection. Anything less than perfection is deemed unworthy; a curse.

Photos are edited repeatedly until the faces captured in the film are no longer recognizable. Music is tuned and auto tuned in studios, creating unrealistic expectations of music when we hear it live. We as citizens of this era are expected to obtain perfection or fail publicly. All of this likely sat as heavy in your mind as it did mine as you painstakingly sat in your doctor's office waiting for a diagnosis.

Sitting on an eggplant colored couch, the seams and cushions worn and the edges beginning to tatter, I sat as far back as the couch itself would let me. My doctor sat across from me, her thin, dainty fingers tapping the keyboard frantically and her eyes repeatedly glancing over to me. The glances were glances of concern, as if she was to look away from me for too long that I would become broken, or more broken than I was.

The anxiety from several continuous days of doctor's appointments, hot tears staining my cheeks and ruining my mascara and the simple fear of the unknown had created a pit in my stomach. It was as if I had eaten a rock and it was sitting just below my belly button. It weighed as heavy as my mind as I listened to the tapping of the keyboard and the clicking of the old clock on the wall.

There was nothing more that I wanted than for her to give me an easy diagnosis, anxiety that I just wasn't dealing with, or even better, a diagnosis of nothing at all. A heave of defeat left my lips as the doctor faced me, her knees nearly touching mine. "This sounds way too much like Bipolar Disorder to ignore your symptoms. We're going to have to try some meds, but I cannot in good faith *not* diagnose you as Bipolar."

The words hung heavy on my mind as I silently drove home in the darkness of the cold January evening. My emotions were torn. The entirety of my adult life I suspected something was wrong with me, but the official diagnosis hurt more than I expected. All of the times I had been called 'crazy' or 'psycho' suddenly didn't feel like an insult, but an identifier of myself. It was within that car ride on the way home that I came to the understanding that Bipolar Disorder wasn't a part of a diagnosis that could go away with time, it was who I was.

I was Bipolar. I *am* Bipolar.

Whether you have been diagnosed for five years or five days, I want you to know that I understand you, Beautiful Bipolar.

What followed was nothing less than a roller coaster, but it allowed me to understand so much about myself, about my life. And now that this is hindsight and something I can finally live with, this allows me to understand you.

There were long nights, where sleep was unobtainable. Usually, following those were long days with tear filled eyes and questions about my own life and my survival until sundown. There was an asininely long trial and error process with my medications, allergies to most of them, and trips to the emergency room with the others. Euphoric mania made me question the severity of my diagnosis at all, and the long impossible lows made me question my own life's value. Mood swings happened at any time and without cause or warning.

I didn't understand it then, but I surely do now. I have been there, and I am still there. Beautiful Bipolar, I understand you and that is why I am writing this for you.

You may be feeling overwhelmed by your diagnosis, and that is perfectly fine. This is an overwhelming diagnosis. It is an enormous stress to be sitting in a doctor's office and be told that your brain has what the world knows as an 'invisible illness.' Your stomach churns as you are handed multiple orange pill bottles with those damn safety locking white cap lids. Your brain feels as if it's been replaced by a brick as you are handed stacks of paperwork about your appointments, and pamphlets crammed full of education about your illness.

I recall the immense stress from beginning the process of treatment; feeling so stressed and anxious that I had simply become numb. Many hours during the process of treatment have been spent in such a place of overwhelming anxiety that I have sat silently, staring blankly at white, empty walls and allowing my brain to run wild while I absorb all the information my brain was sending out. Often, it felt as if a hummingbird was in my brain, the buzz of its tiny wings creating chaos inside of my mind and draining all of my energy as I did the only thing I could do, sit silently.

It is difficult to be sitting in a therapist's office and be expected to talk about every aspect of your life with a total stranger. It feels almost insulting to share an office with professionals who seem to have their shit together all too well, while you sit across from them, a blubbering and grotesque mess sits and confesses all of their broken flaws.

This diagnosis is nothing less than overpowering. But please do not fear, Beautiful Bipolar. Because it can and will get better. You, just like every other hero, have a large quest ahead of you.

You may be feeling broken, feeling as if the diagnosis you have is keeping you low and trapped under a dark and rumbling thunderous cloud that is your mind. Hot tears will feel as familiar as the warm drops of summer rain, and your mood will feel like dark clouds, hanging low in the morning following a treacherous storm. The humid fog of your medications will leave you feeling anything but yourself until it is the right medications, and the real rain will do nothing to help your mood. You may be feeling that this may never be fixed and that this storm inside your brain is more of a hurricane that will leave nothing safe and sound.

You are not broken. For centuries, humans have been taking the broken and creating mosaics and other breathtaking works of art. Give yourself time to be broken, and then allow yourself to evolve into the mosaic of your mind and become an even more beautiful work of art than you were originally slated to become.

You likely are feeling physically ill. Every cycle actually does make most Bipolar patients I know ill, and with good medical reason. You cannot go for days without sleep, with insanely high levels of energy without the crash to follow. Your immune system and your mood wears down and you become more prone to illnesses.

When you're depressed your body reacts to that as well, my body choosing to be so full of pain and exhaustion from my mania that I can barely function. Fatigue takes over my ability to leave my bed, headaches and migraines sitting heavy on my forehead and blinding me and abdominal issues that follow a manic bout tend to prevent me from doing much of anything. Tending to my body is necessary and important, but keeps my moods low and depressive. It is such a frustrating experience, but it is all a part of the diagnosis. Beautiful Bipolar, please take care of your body. Sleep as you need it, eat as well as you can and rest whenever your body calls for it.

Embrace your Bipolar Disorder. Own it. However you choose to cope with it, cope with pride and with strength. Your brain is strong and beautiful and unique. Beautiful Bipolar, I'd like to offer you some advice; after ten years of trials and errors I feel as if I can share anything to help you through this, I'd like to.

The first step I'd suggest in beginning your journey to wellness is to let those close to you know about your diagnosis. This is one of the scariest steps you can take. Some families will understand and embrace you, filling your soul with love and support. Other families will react as mine did, informing me that mental illness doesn't exist and living in denial of the diagnosis at all. It is difficult, but trust me when I say this, they need to know.

Invite your family and friends to be a part of your treatment. If you feel comfortable enough to do so, invite them to your therapy sessions or to come to medication evaluations. Allow them to ask you and your care providers questions. Inform your family when you have changes in your medications, tell them what medications you are on, and be open when you tell them how you are doing.

In my own experiences, I had found that many times I thought I was doing well it was the opposite. Through the help of my family and friends and them being a part of my treatment, I was able to get back on the right track.

By allowing those in your life in on your secret is not only advocating for yourself, but you are bravely advocating for the nearly six million other Americans that suffer from this. I'm sure this diagnosis makes you feel so alone, yet you are in a sea of survivors and thrivers also living with this. Be the person that stands up bravely, fighting for your own life and for the lives of others. There is safety in numbers. I firmly believe we can all save each others lives if we can just stand up and speak up.

The biggest benefit to allowing those in your life to know what you are going through is the simple ability for them to understand. For years, my family and friends could not understand me or my behaviors. Honestly, I was a mystery to them.

They could not understand why I'd say yes to a midnight road trip across the state, but the next week I could not leave my bed for days. My family could not understand why I was spring cleaning my home at two in the morning, yet I could not make it to bridal showers or other events a few days later. My co workers could not figure out why I was such a hard worker most days, but other days I could barely keep my eyes open. Questions about my behaviors were met with tears, or even hostility and rage. No one knew, and no one could possibly have understood. Once I allowed them to know what I was going through I was finally met with what I needed; understanding, compassion and the ability to actually care for myself.

Beautiful Bipolar, you are going to need to find a healthy method for coping with all of this. There are many options and methods I have seen. Some people are quite solemn and serious, giving the facts and figures and allowing the world to see the severity of the situation. I've even met a Bipolar or two that deflect their disorder and channel their mania and their depression into other things, like their children or a hobby. While this can be incredibly healthy, I've seen this become incredibly dangerous as well. As for me, I choose to chase the humor in this otherwise humorless situation. There is something that feels so special to me about being able to make jokes about myself and my diagnosis; allowing others to know that I am not only aware of it, but that I am able to own my shit. I do everything in my power to control the situation and the silliness and absurdity of it all.

I'm going to reiterate my original piece of advice.

Please, take care of yourself first and foremost. It is not heroic to sacrifice yourself for others. Instead, put yourself first so you can be there more often and in a more positive light.

If you need help with getting yourself in order with work, consider applying for the Federal Medical Leave of Absence Act (FMLA). By applying for this and using it myself I was able to take sick days due to medication reactions and while I got myself in order. Days where I was crashing from a manic high to a depressive low changed. Before, I would push through a work day while resenting myself and my coworkers, nothing got done for any of us and the hostility was palpable. Now I am able to tell them the truth, and when I need a day to better myself and take my meds, I take it. Work has become a pleasant place again and I am able to do more for myself and my co workers.

If you have children and need help, do not hesitate to ask your significant other or other family members for help, even if it's for a few hours. I was hesitant to do this at first, wondering how it would damage the relationship with my son. However, instead of our relationship being damaged, my husband and son now have a wonderful relationship with each other. While mom is down for the day or the afternoon and needs to focus on herself, dad is able to take him to baseball games, or movies, or even in the backyard to play soccer. Instead of mom crying uncontrollably or yelling at a little boy who doesn't deserve it, I am able to take my medications and when I am able to join them, I do happily.

Beautiful Bipolar, there is so much you can do once you figure out how to live with this diagnosis. Many Bipolar patients have found ways to channel their thoughts, emotions and feelings into beautiful creations.

Artists like Van Gogh have been able to use the paintbrush to project the workings of his mind, while Actors like Catherine Zeta-Jones has been able to use her skills on the silver screen to project those overwhelming emotions we face. Jean-Claude Van Damme used kickboxing as an outlet to his mania, meanwhile Demi Lovato chooses music as her outlet of choice. All of these people have created beautiful things, and all while being 'sick' with Bipolar Disorder.

Find what drives you, Beautiful Bipolar. Find what eases the pain that your soul feels. Delve deep into dirty soil, getting the grit of the earth underneath your fingernails. Allow your favorite jeans to be stained by the splatter of acrylic paint. Allow your fingertips to become calloused from the nylon strings of a guitar. Travel aimlessly throughout your hometown and find the perfect places to capture photos or film videos. Feed your brain and that beautiful bipolar soul; you're going to create beautiful work that will speak to the world.

This book is written for you. This is the book that my own soul craved through every moment of my diagnosis, my treatment and now through my survival.

While this seems by this essay that this is a self-help book, it is not. I am not here to tell you how to survive, I am here to tell you that I understand what you are going through. I am here to share my stories and how I tried to thrive, but many times failed and barely survived.

As you read these pages, I want you to know that you are not alone. You will survive the storm that is raging inside your mind. Beautiful Bipolar, this isn't a curse, this is the gift of enhanced creativity and intelligence.

There is no cure for Bipolar disorder, but there are some treatments that may work. So revel in your highs and treat your lows. Be as beautiful as your brain is.

"It's not fair. It's not fair that I live with this. It's not fair that my brain does this. It's not fair that my family is fucked up. It's not fair that they put their problems onto me. It's fucked up that fucked up things happened. It's not fair to deal with this all at once. It hurts."
Journal Entry 7/2/15

"When I see photos of myself as a child and then see myself now, I feel as if I've betrayed myself by being mentally ill."
Journal Entry 7/21/15

"It takes a lot of balls to be mentally ill. It takes a certain type of heroism."
-Carrie Fisher

"There is something wrong with me and I am scared that they won't find a fix for it in time. I'm scared of losing my life before we can find anything - a cure, a medication, a fix, anything. I feel crazy. I feel like I've wasted so much time. I'm tired. My husband is tired. Everyone is tired, and I wonder if it is even worth it anymore. I want to feel loved. I feel like maybe that can get me through this. I just need to feel like I am worth more than just my illness."
Journal Entry 7/11/15

Midnight Devastation

We had shared our hearts with each other for twelve short months, and shared walls and a bed for six. We had shared laughs, and tears. We had shared road trips and adventures in the bedroom. We even had the promise of sharing the rest of our lives sitting on my left hand's fourth finger. Most days that promise gave me a glimmer of hope in an otherwise dreary world, but not tonight. Tonight that promise weighed heavy on my hand and I felt the pain of a lovers quarrel.

Our bedroom was small and cramped. Cheap furniture and old memories our childhoods filled the room and in the middle of it laid the only thing we had purchased together, our bed. I sat on the edge of it while he stood by the door. A light blue light escaped through the curtains and cast an eerie gray glow into the room. The music we had previously been listening to was drown out by our voices.

The words exchanged between us didn't matter. We weren't even listening to what the other was saying anyways. I felt betrayed by him and his actions, and in his eyes I could see he shared the feeling too. The pain was too much, and I reacted in the only way that I knew how. I went in for the verbal kill. Yelling, I said things that were completely unfair and untrue. In response to my allegations, he turned and left our basement apartment, slamming the door loudly behind him. The slamming of the door rattled the walls and our engagement photo slid from its place on the wall onto the floor, the glass shattering with it.

Hot tears filled my eyes and I stared at the ceiling as I tried to blink them away. A sharp feeling sat in the base of my throat, as if I had stubbed my little toe and I couldn't yell out in pain. It was as if my body betrayed me and with a loud sniff, the tears began to freely trickle down my cheeks. Under my sternum I could feel my heart galloping as it took off with my emotions. My body began to feel frigid from the pure adrenaline. It was as if pure, thick ice was trying to pound through my veins. The thick fingers of panic wrapped itself around my neck and the more I tried to breathe, the more difficult it became. Placing my own hand on my neck, I fell back onto our bed. I wanted to scream, but I was physically unable to do so.

Anxiety filled my mind, racing thoughts taking off from the deepest corners of my mind and escaping rapidly. The escapees of my mind created havoc in my consciousness and created fear that spread into my heart.

The longer I sat silently, the worse it became. Without someone to distract me or stop me from sitting in the chaos, My mind was free to do whatever it wanted.

Leaning over to my fiancee's bedside table I pulled open the drawer. My vision was blurred, as if I was moving too fast to catch clear vision. Without a pause for hesitation I leaned into the top drawer and pulled out his leather-man tool. Frantically, breathing heavily I pulled it open, picking at the tools rapidly. I could not even stall myself before I began to rapidly hack at my wrists.

Each hack across my wrist stung sharply as the tiny knife of the leather-man embedded into my wrist. A sense of contentment and disgust overtook me as I looked at my wrist each time. I wasn't bleeding like I thought I would. "Up stream. Not across the street." I whispered to myself, referring to the slang terms used to describe the type of cuts used by psychiatric patients in the hospitals. "Up the stream."

Lifting the leather-man again, turning the blade to face up my arm, the cut aimed to go from my wrist to my elbow, I inhaled sharply. As I slowly pressed the blade deep into my wrist the sting of the blade caused me to pause.

As quickly as I picked up the leather-man I tossed it aside, my right arm stinging and starting to bleed. Bright red blood trickled down my arm towards my elbow and as I studied it I lost all composure I had held for that brief moment and began to sob. Burying my face into my hands and making disgusting noises as I tried to breathe and stop crying at the same time.

It took a few minutes to be able to settle myself down enough to regain composure, but I was able to do so. Sitting on the bed, my knees pressed tightly against my chest and my hand on my forehead I sighed, feeling overwhelmed and defeated.

Over the course of the last six months so much had happened in our lives. I had quit going to school full time and picked up more shifts at the hospital I worked at. I began working fifty hour weeks taking care of psychiatric and medical surgical patients. It was necessary so that I could financially support my fiance so he could attend the police academy and obtain his lifelong dream of being a police officer.

At first I tested into the Paramedic program that was my lifelong dream, but after the first medication test and a follow up physical fitness test found that it was all too much to handle. I failed out of the program.

Throughout the course of all of the drama between my fiance and I, there was drama in my childhood home as well. They were unhappy with my 'life choices', and that I wasn't living the exact way they wanted me to. One evening my mother and I were bickering and I told her I was going to go to my fiance's home. She was upset and texted my phone non stop, so I messaged her in return and told her that I was going to turn my phone off for a bit and that I would be home an hour before my already early curfew. A few hours later, when I went to turn on my phone I found about twenty messages and even more missed calls and voice mails. As I checked them I saw one from my father. '*Your shit is on the porch. Come get it and get out of my house.*'

It had been dramatic moment after moment and in the midst of all the craziness I craved stability and sanity. I missed my home. I missed my family. I was heartbroken to see that they were no longer speaking to me. During this time, I felt like an inconvenience to my fiance and his family, who had kindly accepted and adopted me into their life. Because of my hurt feelings, I hardly left the apartment.

During all this time I hadn't thought to pause to care for myself. However, that pause would mean that I needed to admit that I was struggling, and that was the last thing I wanted to do.

Sniffing and wiping my hand under my nose, my eyes fell from the wall in front of me to the large bottle of Tylenol sitting on my bedside table. Years ago I had injured my shoulder and since then I suffered from subsequent dislocations on a daily basis. The doctors offered me opioids, but I refused, only allowing myself to take Tylenol for the pain and discomfort until my surgery later in the year. My left hand fell from my forehead to my side as it slowly drifted over to the top drawer of my bedside table, pulling it open with my fingertips. My knees fell to my side as I leaned forward to peek.

Inside the drawer was all of my medications that I ever had taken or been prescribed. There was Benadryl, Lorazepam and a few leftover Tramadol pills from my shoulder injection a few weeks back. Inhaling sharply I looked at all of the medications, the orange and white pill bottles lined up in an orderly manner. In my chest my heart continued to pound, the sound echoing in my ears. Meanwhile my body felt numb, the only feeling I could identify was nausea.

My family likely would not want to do an autopsy, but my fiance would. After the battle of doing one at all was won, it would take weeks to do. Likely the conclusion they'd jump to is that it was an accidental overdose. Once the report was released they would fight about what to do with my body. During all of this though, I'd be long gone and their decisions would be worthless.

When you suffer from a Tylenol overdose, you suffer from multi-system organ failure. Unfortunately this would mean that you could not donate my body for science. The body would be just a shell, leaving everything worthless. The best option for my family would be to cremate me, which is what I wanted for myself anyways. I suppose they'd use that as their excuse for doing that at all, keeping the fights and disputes to themselves. With the autopsy report they'd never know that it was an accomplished suicide attempt. They would never have to deal with me ever again. They would never have to see me this low or this depressed ever again.

Hot tears were flowing freely from my eyes again and blurring my vision. It was not like this was a new experience or feeling, deep down I always known that I was mentally ill. Truthfully, I had known for years.

When I was eighteen years old I had my first mental lapse. It was a terrifying experience and immediately afterwards I was placed for help. I was placed on half a dozen psychiatric medications and placed into religious therapy. My father advised me to put up a front and fight through it. During the hours of sitting in the office covered in wood paneling, I lied to the therapist. I told him what he wanted to hear. He sucked as a therapist anyways, he believed the bullshit I said to him.

In the years following I had been on and off of medications with no success. The side effects always outweighed the benefits and I was taken off of them quickly. In the past I had been low enough to sedate myself or distract myself to avoid lapses again. Not tonight, tonight was a new low, a low I had never felt before.

Lying back onto the bed, I looked up to the fan on the ceiling. "This isn't going to go away." I whispered to myself, feeling defeated. "This is incurable."

It was as if I had no physical control over my body as I quickly sat up and turned to my fiance's dresser to my left. On top of it was an open can of now flavorless and flat Coke, and without a second thought I grabbed it. My left hand already had grabbed the large bottle of Tylenol and was pouring the contents of the bottle out onto our comforter.

Lifting the can to my lips I paused. '*Bottoms up.*' I thought, then swallowed a handful of the pills with a swig of the soda.

Two handfuls of pills went down easily before I paused to pick up my cell phone. I tried to do the math on how many pills I actually needed to take. My stomach churned, the feeling that I may throw up sat in the back of my throat. Clenching my fist against my lips I swallowed and shook my head. I began feeling like I was going to hyperventilate, but with each gasp for air I felt more nauseated than before. Opening the Lorazepam, I poured out some onto the bed, trying to calm my nerves. My hands shook and three pills fell out of the bottle instead of the one I wanted to take. I closed my eyes and put all three of them in my mouth. I felt so incredibly nauseated but at peace with my decision.

According to a quick Google search I found that seven thousand milligrams of Tylenol is what will kill you. That is fourteen pills of the extra strength Tylenol to make it happen - which in this situation is nothing. Another Google search found that no one really knows how many Benadryl pills it would take. As I searched, my thumb scrolling the poor quality web pages, I took a few more pills.

The effects of the medications hit fairly quickly, and I had to stumble around the bedroom to get myself cleaned up. I grabbed the cool sheets on the bed, turning it down. The corner of the bed folded down like you would see in a catalog or a nice hotel. The cotton sheets felt good between my fingers, but I couldn't pause to appreciate it, I had to keep moving before all those medications kicked into effect.

I then put on a clean pair of pajamas. Usually, I wore trashy short shorts and a tank top, but tonight I put on a cute pajama set I had received for Christmas the year before. The plaid pants felt warm as I put them on, and the tank top felt clean and new against my bare skin. Straightening them out, I nodded to myself in approval.

Finally I pulled my hair up into a high bun on top of my head. I turned off the music that was blaring over the radio and turned on the television, I needed noise to calm my nerves. With a relieved sigh that I was ready, I collapsed back into the bed. My brain started to become as drowsy and limp as my body felt, barely able to think. As I began to drift off into unconsciousness, a quote crossed my mind, something a therapist had told me. "You're mentally ill. You'll either die with it or because of it."

"Come on!" A voice yelled. I winced awake. My vision was blurred, I could barely make out light as I tried to look around. An intense pain stung my chest, it felt like an exceptionally large bee sting over my sternum. "Dani! Wake up!"

The room began to take shape again the more my

eyes focused on it. The blobs of light slowly began the shapes and outlines of my apartment and of my fiance. Another sharp sting and I realized what he was doing. He was rubbing his knuckles against my sternum, a typical first responder move to check for level of consciousness. We'd do it to each other from time to time as we play fought or tormented each other, but I knew he was nowhere near playing.

I tried to speak, tried to respond to his yelling. I could not. I felt lifeless and empty as I laid there. The Benadryl had dried up my nose, leaving my tongue feeling like sandpaper. The Lorazepam kept taking over my clear vision and blurring my world up again. And the Tylenol took whatever pain I was feeling before and embalmed me in a numb feeling.

"Blink if you can hear me." My fiance pleaded. I did blink, slowly, my eyes feeling as if they were impossible to open again. He sighed and stopped, hanging his head. "What did you do?" He whispered, his hand gripping mine. I wanted to respond so badly, but physically could not. As I laid there, feeling like a vegetable, my eyes drifted shut and I started to drift back into darkness. He shook me again, this time forcefully sharking me by my shoulders. "Tell me what to do here!" He yelled. "Do I let you sleep? Do I take you to the hospital? What do I do?"

My body was numb, but I tried to nod. I couldn't even feel the pressure of his hands against my arms. My breathing was becoming more and more shallow and it felt as if even my lungs were becoming sleepy.

For the first time in years I felt at peace. As I drifted back off I realized that I was truly okay with my decision. I forced myself to speak to my fiance. "I'm trying to die." I whispered.

The sun peeked through the curtains, the air conditioner blowing the vinyl blinds and causing them to tap together. My body ached as I laid in bed. Slowly, I began to move, trying to see what else I could feel besides pain.

Devastated. It was the only thing I could think of as my mind started to come back to consciousness. I felt as I had already failed at everything in life, and now I could add ending my life to my list of failures. Not only that, but I had devastated my fiance, who was lying next to me, tightly clutching my body. My eyes fell to the clock on the bedside table. I was scheduled to go to work in a few hours and take care of people, who like me had tried to kill themselves last night.

I was devastated that I had to continue living with this monster in my head. I was devastated that the monster had evolved into something much, much worse than it was before.

My fiance stirred awake. I dropped my head onto his shoulder and sighed, trying not to cry. "Hi." I whispered to him, my voice dry and raspy.

"You tried to die." He whispered back, tucking himself tighter into me.

"Yes. I tried to die." I repeated back to him.

"You almost died last night."

"I almost died."

"There is something that happens when someone finds out that you are mentally ill. There is a moment - and no matter who it is, their faces are the same. At first, it is concern. A fall in the eyes, sadness, pity. The attempt to understand visually what is going on, and if you look well visually, well it is awful. Then there is the disbelief. You look well, say "I'm doing okay," but don't look messed up, so they don't believe it. Then comes the questions. The awful poking and prodding."
Journal Entry 8/1/15

"I feel inadequate. I feel overwhelmed. My counselor says I am entitled to these feelings, but I still feel guilty for having them. From previous therapy sessions I know that this is a parental voice, being internally spoken through me. His verbal dissent over the years has become my internal dictation of myself. And it fucking sucks."
Journal Entry, January, 2015

"I can tell I'm swinging high towards mania again because I don't feel like I'm living. I feel frozen in life - like I've done nothing in the last ten years. I want to be educated. I want to swim in oceans. I want to sing and not care. I want to be like those girl in the stock inspirational photos. Beautiful, mysterious, interesting. Instead, I feel like a blob of doom and gloom. Like gum stuck to the bottom of a shoe, no matter how much you try to get rid of it, it'll never be all the way gone."
Journal Entry 8/4/15

Road Trip

"I was so blissfully happy doing nothing." This is the general idea that Elizabeth Gilbert tries to give us as she's reading Eat. Pray. Love. over my stereo system. I sighed and shook my head, turning the CD off and turning the radio on instead. I'd tried so many times to read this book on CD, and each time was met feeling the same reactions towards it.

The first reaction was anger. It was an easy to read book, which made me so inexplicably upset. Perhaps it was because I usually read the classics, Dickens, Chaucer, Shakespeare, Thoreau, Frost, and had recently and regretfully branched into current non-fiction novels. This book felt too easy to listen to, and often instead of listening to it, I'd drift off and let my brain take over, re-creating ways I'd word her sentences or even rewriting the whole chapter. Being spoiled by authors like David Sedaris and A.J. Jacobs, I was disgusted that anyone had published this novel. Worse, Julia Roberts agreed to act in the motion picture production of it. Pretty Woman, no more.

The next reaction trailed so closely behind anger like the train of a wedding gown. Annoyance. I couldn't help but think 'oh boo fucking hoo,' so many times while angrily shutting it off. She got a divorce, so what? I was beaten, left behind and divorced at a far younger age, and I didn't go sobbing about it and losing fifty pounds. I did what any real woman would do, I got up, put on my boxing gloves and got the fuck over it, waiting for the next punch and stronger than before. But no, Elizabeth Gilbert, the whiny woman she is, had to travel the world to go find herself. I suppose when the world you live in is sick of hearing of your depression then you do run away to new countries.

Ms. Gilbert, if you're reading this, I'd like to offer you a suggestion. Next time you talk about depression and being scared of hurting yourself, you might want to actually have those problems. I don't for one moment believe you almost cut yourself. As someone who once didn't believe she would do it, and when I was truly depressed did cut, I find it insulting. Why include it in your novel at all? All you did was ensure that you insulted 14.8 million depressed adults.

The final reaction that gets me to shut off the book that is depleting my brain cells is the narcissism of her stories. "Oh look at me as I speak Italian." The story goes.

"Look at me as I eat all this amazing food." Two minutes in and I slap the FM/AM button on the stereo so hard that I could be charged with assault if anyone saw it.

"Fuck you." I mutter.

The only part of the story that I liked was when she realized she hadn't been truly happy in a while. Not that I like anyone's misery or unhappiness, but it made me think about the simplicity of happiness and to ponder my own.

Happiness is so interesting to me. The concept of being happy doing nothing is actually something I know well, some of my fondest memories include having no schedule and nothing to do besides simply be in the moment. My husband comes from a large family, with a to-do list so extensive and busy that since we've been together those moments of pure happiness are farther and fewer between.

It was a spring afternoon when I decided I had enough. I was young, barely nineteen, and the weight of the world on my shoulders was weighing me down. The pain of the stress was making me feel weak, the overwhelming emotions cursing me. The anniversary of my best friend and my grandfather's death had just passed, finals were coming up for spring semester, and I was planning a wedding while my fiance was away with the military. Looking in the mirror, I felt overwhelmed. Studying myself I felt sick to my stomach, unable to recognize myself as I studied my blue eyes and touched my cheek. Frustrated with myself I leaned in closer to the mirror, trying to make my brain connect. "Screw this." I said, standing up and tossing the wedding magazine I had been looking at on my bed.

I looked around my room, studying everything. The room was perfectly tidy, everything in its place, everything where it ought to be. Turning back to the mirror I looked at myself, I was dressed nicely in a button up blouse and a nice pair of jeans. While it all looked the way I'm sure it ought to, I was suddenly upset. This wasn't me.

Putting on my blue jeans with the hole in the knee and my cowboy boots made me feel a little better, but it wasn't until I put on my old blue tee shirt and a hoodie that I finally felt comfortable. I turned and looked at myself in the mirror, but instead of admiring my more natural look, I watched myself grab my bag and leave.

There are two streets that take you from downtown Salt Lake to just about anywhere you'd want to be. State Street and Redwood Road. Both of which stretch down south into the next county. I grabbed a bottle of water and an old CD mix that a friend had made me and drove down Redwood road, south bound. The radio was blaring, so loud that I couldn't hear my own voice over it. Outside my window the suburbs of Salt Lake county passed me by and I felt so free leaving it all behind.

Saratoga Springs is about thirty minutes outside of town, a perfect crossroads to stop. East takes you to Lehi, South takes you down past Utah lake and a half a dozen small towns, and West takes you to Eagle Mountain. Approaching the single stoplight that was in that town I saw a grocery store and knew I had to stop.

My boots clicking against the tile I walked into the store. I wandered the store aimlessly, searching for what I could have possibly stopped for, when I saw it. Jones Soda, the kind in the glass bottle, Strawberry Kiwi flavored. I grabbed two and a power-bar and headed to the checkout.

Leaning against my car in the parking lot I opened up the first Jones bottle and smiled as I took a sip. I sat up on the trunk of my Volkswagen and studied the sunset as the sun started to slowly fall behind the mountains in the west. The colors were so incredibly vibrant, oranges, yellows, reds. It was a classic Utah sunset, and it was gorgeous.

'It's going to be okay.' I told myself, sipping on my soda. 'It's got to be okay.'

Once my bottle was depleted I returned behind the wheel and turned over the ignition again. It was warm out, and once I started towards the East, I rolled my window down and let in a deep breath. The warm wind, the smell of the grass and manure, the farmland and ranches now surrounding me, it was all perfect.

Halfway to Lehi I stopped and pulled the car over, admiring a herd of horses as they stood at the fence, watching the cars go by. They were gorgeous creatures, standing tall and nearly majestic in the sunset light. The dusk was creating a beautiful light on them and I sat in awe, not wanting to move in fear of spooking them.

In our suburb neighborhood we actually had a lot of families with horses. West Jordan was originally a farming and ranching town when it first came into play, and those who moved in first bought it with the idea of ranching and farming. So many lots were still just that, and within our neighborhood we had a few neighbors with horses. On warm nights my dad and I would go for walks and go visit those properties, watching them run and play, or, if we were lucky, they'd come to us and let us touch them. There was something so wonderful about those visits to see them, and even when my dad and I quit walking together, I'd search them out.

The moment your fingertips touch the mane of a horse is a blissful moment. In those moments when this large, strong, respected creature chooses to trust you and you reach out, something happens to your soul. It's almost as if they're telling you that you're okay, and those large brown eyes bore into your soul, they're reading you like a book.

The fall before I had gone walking to clear my mind. I was stressed from midterms, work, and all the drama that comes with being eighteen years old. I put on my running shoes and headed on the familiar three mile walk that my dad and I had mapped out. I had my own pit stops and pauses mapped along the way and wanted to get outside and move. I sprinted up the street to my first stop, the large farm at the top of the street, where acres of land was still rural and free. Halfway through I found myself standing next to Boris' land. Boris, was my favorite horse, a tall, strong, chocolate brown beauty that was always so friendly when I came to visit. Whenever I'd arrive he'd greet me with a loud 'pffft' and always let me greet him with an outstretched hand. Most horses would get spooked if I'd say anything, but Boris didn't mind. In fact, it was as if he wanted me to talk to him, he'd stand still and stare at me.

When I got to his land we said our hello's like always, but this time I couldn't find the words to speak. After a few moments of touching his mane and looking to him I sighed. "I'm sorry, I don't know." I said shakily. A tear rolled down my cheek and I sighed, embarrassed. Here I was, crying to a horse.

I'd only seen horses hug humans in movies, when you know there's a carrot hanging overhead or some other bribe. I'd heard stories and seen photos, but I'd never seen it in real life. As I tried to step away from Boris, suddenly his head was pushing into me, pushing me as close to him as the fence separating us would allow. I sighed and smiled, patting his chest and giving into this hug. He 'pfft'ed again and I giggled, suddenly understanding all of those corny cowboy movies where the cowboys are so in love with these horses. As he looked to me, he licked his teeth, making him look as if he was smiling at me.

"Hey guys." I said, getting out of my car and

studying the horses that stood there. There were about five of them, and they were moving their eyes between me and between the road. I pulled my soda out of the car and sat on the trunk again, just sitting and watching. A semi drove by loudly and the horses scattered, running rampantly around their field. I watched them in awe, the sound of their hoof beats all I could hear. It was beautiful.

I was sitting by myself, a soda bottle in my hands and a dead cell phone in my car. I was far enough away from home to worry my family but close enough to get away from it all. Garth Brooks was singing to me from the radio in my car, and the gallop of the horses was like a sedative for my soul. In the orange and yellow of the last light of the day, I studied them. It was the most perfect moment, and for that brief moment, I was happy.

So blissfully happy doing nothing.

"There was once a time when I thought being an adult meant choking down emotions and toughing it out. Turns out, it's quite the opposite. It's owning your emotions, discussing those nagging feelings and being real about shit."
-Journal Entry, 1/12/16

"I say everything because it's all bullshit. People take things too fucking seriously. If you get offended by bullshit, what you're offended by is the least of your problems."
-Ru Paul

"The book I want to write (or really, the book I need to write) is the tale of a girl who survived. Despite all dysfunction, despite the bipolar disorder, despite the neurotic tendencies, despite all of the obstacles in may way - I survived. Other people need to know that they, too, can survive."
- Journal Entry 2/29/16

Crazy

I knew I was awake before I could open my eyes. My eyelids felt so incredibly heavy, like they were sewn shut, and my legs ached as I tried to stretch them. I fought with all my senses as I tried to regain consciousness. The air smelled stale, the scent reminded me of dirty laundry. My fingertips inched their way over the blankets that laid over my body, the thin, ratted blankets that I always slept with. Voices spoke in the distance, but because they were muffled I could tell there was a closed door between us. My mouth was dry, my tongue rough like sandpaper. After a few moments of using my other senses, I could start to open my eyes. First it was a blurry, pale light, but before too long I was able to make out the shapes and furniture of my bedroom.

Lying on my back, I could only stare at the ceiling. My mind raced as I laid completely still. Questions flew through my mind, my brain felt like a tornado, both destructive and fast-paced. I had no idea how I had gotten to my bed - the last I knew I was in my truck, my boyfriend was with me at the time. My head fell to my right and my eyes fell onto my arms, which were covered in small bruises, no bigger than a pencil eraser. On my forearm was a long, brown and yellow bruise from an IV. By the colors of the bruise and how faded it appeared it looked to be at least three or four days old, but the last I could remember, I had the IV placed yesterday and it was a deep purple and blue bruise.

Feeling scared and slightly panicked, I sat up, pressing my back against the wall for stability. I studied my bedroom, my head heavy and feeling dizzy. Everything sat immaculate, and nothing looked out of place. I was able to conclude that I had to not have been up and moving much if nothing was out of its place. Sighing, my eyes fell to the large mirror on the dresser across from my bed and studied myself.

Holy shit, I was a mess. My hair was pulled up into a high and messy bun on top of my head. My makeup had either been washed off or smeared off, but remnants of eyeliner and mascara lined my eyes, creating a smokey train wreck look. My nail polish was chipped and my lips were so chapped they were starting to bleed as I moved them. My eyes physically hurt, my bladder was full, weighing down heavily on me as I already struggled to move. Despite all my best efforts, I couldn't bring myself to move any more than I already had, I felt so overwhelmed by how physically numb I felt and the

54

whirlwind of emotions racing through my mind. I had no recollection of how I got here.

We sat on the hood of my Ford Bronco. The roughness of the Bondo and chipped paint was rough under my hand as I leaned back onto it. Sean and I sat side by side, talking.

The truck was parked in an elementary school parking lot, a safe place for both of us since the incident. As we spoke we couldn't bring ourselves to look to each other, instead our eyes fell to the ground or ahead of us.

"You went crazy." Sean said, studying his Jones soda bottle. He picked at the label with his fingernails as he continued. "I mean, that night I met up with your ex he said you were crazy, but that…" He scoffed. "That was crazy."

"I know." I said quietly, studying the asphalt. "And you know how much I hate that you two met up…" I took a swig from my soda bottle, the sticky sweet taste of strawberry kiwi providing a small relief from the painful conversation. "I don't know what happened." I admitted, feeling ashamed of myself.

Sean's legs swing off the hood of my truck like a children's swing set, swinging forward and backward wildly. He stopped the swinging of his legs to spit on the ground and then shook his head. "You went crazy." He repeated.

With a sigh, I laid back and onto the windshield.

My bottle in one hand and my other hand on my belt buckle, my eyes studied the sky. If that's what we wanted to call it, then sure, I suppose I went crazy. I sure wasn't sane, but I surely didn't feel crazy. Crazy is defined as mentally deranged, and as I laid there, studying the clouds, I didn't feel like a mentally deranged person.

It was an abnormally cool night, the summer breeze blew softly through the rolled down windows of Sean's truck as we drove. The sun was setting behind us, the orange glow of last light filled the sky.

"You're acting strange." Sean said.

"It's because I want to go home." I admitted. "I want life to go back to the way it was." Not long after graduation I was asked to leave my parents home, and Sean and his family graciously took me in. It had been a month of squatting at their home and I wanted nothing more than to go back to my parents home, to go back to my own bedroom, my own bed. "I think I want to break up."

The gas pedal hit the floor of the truck and I flew from the middle seat to the far passenger door as he started to drive worse than usual. My elbow hit the metal door and I yelled out in surprise as I tried to catch myself. Sean was a piss-poor driver as it was, and I expected us to crash as he let his anger take the driver's' seat. Tires screeched as he pulled into our destination - the parking lot of our friends job site. We were going to pick him up from work, and instead we were nearly crashing into the building.

Words were exchanged. I yelled my part. After realizing that it wasn't going anywhere, I got out of the old, beat up truck and walked away.

It was almost total darkness, the vibrant orange sky was now yellow and pale blue and the temperature had dropped even more, and I rubbed my arms briskly to warm up as I walked. Old and dim streetlights were the only lights around and I turned off of the very busy road and into an old neighborhood. We were in what was considered to be the 'bad part' of town, and as I walked into this neighborhood, the small houses and pit bulls behind broken chain link fences seemed comforting compared to the wild truck ride I was just on. I peeked over my shoulder, in the hopes that I wasn't being followed by Sean, or anyone else for that matter.

My footsteps echoed around me as I turned the corner and headed west. In my head I tried to map out where I was going to go. The sound of screeching tires suddenly filled the air and I pressed my back against a wooden fence, panicked and looking for where they came from. Familiar headlights rounded the corner and shone on me, and in fear for my life I started to run.

"Dani!" Sean yelled as he pulled the truck up and onto the sidewalk in front of me. "Get. In." He yelled out to me.

"Sean, just go away!" I yelled back, trying to run around the truck, but as I started to move, he cut me off with the truck, nearly hitting me with it as he pulled forward. "Please!" I pleaded, punching the hood of his truck in anger. The cold feeling of adrenaline filled my veins, pumping through my body.

"Get in the god-damn truck and stop being so stubborn!" He yelled back to me, honking the horn at me as I tried to move.

To my left I noticed there were three rather large Hispanic men sitting on lawn chairs in their front yard. As I looked to them, they stood and started towards us. They wore torn-up white tank tops, their jeans covered in plaster and had holes in them and were covered in tattoos. Normally, I'd be scared of these men but in this moment I felt the urge to run towards them and ask them to save me. Instead of taking my chances, I decided to get tricky and try to save myself.

Starting towards the truck, I reached my hand out towards the truck door handle. The door had to be opened from the inside, so I waited for Sean to lean over to open the door. As he leaned over, I turned to my right and started to sprint away.

At the end of the road was a chain link fence, and past it a chain link fence to a strip mall. My breath heavy as I sprinted, my heart pounded in my chest. I got to the fence as the sound of Sean's truck revved. I climbed the fence to jump it - my shirt getting caught in the fence and tearing. I jumped down, my feet hitting the pavement and kept running, leaving a piece of my shirt on the fence.

As I got to the opposite end of the parking lot he familiar headlights faced me again and I was facing Sean's truck, this time our friend Dan was running up behind me. Desperate and in fear, I saw an auto shop in the west corner of the parking lot and ran towards it, hiding behind a dumpster.

The truck's engine turned off and I could hear the boys talking quietly to each other as I panted, trying to quietly find a way out of this. After a moment, Sean began to yell towards me again. "Dani, get out here before shit gets real."

I slid down the side of the dumpster and sat down on the asphalt, hoping he'd just go away. Instead, he appeared around the corner and stood over me. In my hands I had the torn part of my shirt, playing with it and studying the tear. I had started a new job at a warehouse and had a box cutter in my back pocket, so I took it out and cut the ragged, torn part of the bottom of my shirt off and tossed the fabric and the box cutter aside.

"Sean," I started with a sigh. "I'm done. Please, just take me home."

"No." He said, crossing his arms and tapping his steel toed boot, the sound loud and echoing in the silence that filled us. "I've seen what goes down, I know what this is all about."

"I don't even want my things." I said, hanging my head. "Just please, I want to go home."

"No." He repeated. "Trust me when I say I'm

protecting you, I'm protecting you."

It surely didn't feel like I was being protected. It felt like a murder attempt, the irrational driving, the nearly running me down, the chase scene that just occurred.

"How can I word this so you'll understand it?" I asked loudly, standing up and swinging an arm out to shoo him away. "I don't want to be with you anymore!" I yelled. "I don't love you! I am not happy! I want to go home!" As I yelled, Sean stared towards me, my arms waving with every sentence I spoke, trying to get him to leave me alone. He reached out towards me and I tried to step back, my back hitting the garbage can.

"Sean! Stop it!" I snapped, slapping his arms away. "Stop!" I spit on his shoes and he stopped and stared at me. "I'd rather be dead than continue this relationship!" I screamed.

"Dani?" Dan asked, peeking out from behind the garbage can and looking at us.

"Ugh!" I yelled, then started towards the stores in the strip mall. I hid behind a cement pillar and sat down on the cold ground, the cool night air embracing my bare arms and feeling chilly as I sat. I hung my head and rested my elbows on my knees, hot tears started to form in my eyes and I inhaled shakily, trying to regain any composure I had. I removed my hair from the ponytail it was in and ran my fingers through my hair.

Sirens started ringing out in the cool night air. I sat there, staring into the glass of the closed tax offices in front of me and watched the reflection as the red and blue lights got closer and closer to me. Scared, I stood and pressed myself against the pillar as if to hide myself. Peeking around one corner, I saw Sean leaning against his truck, picking at his fingernails casually. Dan stood next to him, looking to me. By the look on his face alone I could tell they had called the police on me, but I could not figure out why.

"Ms. Donner?" A voice asked. I looked to my left as a uniformed officer approached me. My stomach dropped and I slid to the ground, looking up at him and feeling sick. He adjusted his belt and studied me. "We got a call... sounds like you're having a rough night."

"I didn't know running away from a boy you'd want to break up with is worthy of calling you guys out." I said, rubbing my hand across my forehead.

"It's not, but I heard you were wanting to hurt yourself." He replied.

"The exact words were 'I'd rather be dead than in a relationship with you'." I replied sarcastically. "Figured he'd walk away and just let me be."

"Well, I need you to stand up so we can talk." He said to me, nodding his head. "My partner is over there talking to your...boyfriend?"

"Ex." I replied sharply. The officer gave me a dirty look and I stood, leaning my head back against the pillar. "Sorry," I replied. "You're right, I am having a rough night." The officer nodded and peeked around the pillar.

61

"Looks like you have quite a showing." He said. I peeked around the pillar to see that now Sean was accompanied by his sisters, their spouses and his parents. My parents were pulling up in their car and I sighed, leaning back against the cold cement pillar.

"I just wanted him to take me home and let us be over." I said, moaning as I spoke.

"Well," The officer started, studying me. "Since I got called out we do have to follow protocol." He patted my shoulder. "You don't seem in distress to me, but we have to do what we have to do."

"I can't sign an AMA or anything?" I asked, feeling hopeful. The officer shook his head. "He chased me with his truck." I said. "He almost hit me with it!"

"Ms. Donner, I need you to turn around." The officer said. "I'm going to do a quick pat down and then I'm going to start getting you out of here." I turned around and put my hands on the glass in front of us, just like I had seen in reruns of Cops on television. "Anything that's going to poke me or stick me?" He asked as he started to pat my arms.

"No." I replied. " I had a box cutter from work, but I threw it over by the auto shop." I admitted. The officer patted my shoulders, my sides, each leg.

"You can put your arms down." He said, and as I did I felt a tug on my right arm. "Ms. Donner," He started.

"Dani." I interrupted him, closing my eyes as he tugged my left arm. "Please, if you're going to do this, call

62

me by my first name."

"Dani, I'm putting you in these handcuffs as a part of our protocol. Because you are in no emotional distress currently, my partner and I are going to take you to the hospital to do an evaluation in the emergency room. After they check you out then we can let you go."

He pulled me by the handcuffs behind my back and walked me to his car. As he opened the door, I had a moment to stop and pause and look at the group stair at me. I stared back, a rush of emotions filled me as they stood.

No one was going to free me from the chains of a dead and unwanted relationship. No one was going to try to save me from the moment. No one dared move.

The officer put a hand on my shoulder and the other on the cuffs as he helped me into the car. He partner handed him the paperwork and they shut the door. I sat back into the seat - I was completely caged in, like an animal.

We drove in silence, the sound of the radio chatter all I could hear. My mind started to race. I could freak out, I could start thrashing, and really make the moment worth all of this. The backseat cage was made of metal and I could do some serious damage to myself and make enough noise to scare anyone to death in the process.

I wiggled my arms, my shoulders aching in the cuffs. They were actually loose and as I sat there I wiggled my left hand out of it. I considered pulling myself out of them and handing them to the officer. I considered tightening them for him. Instead, I pulled my hand out and flipped them around to the front of me, inserting my hand into the cuff, wondering if the officer would even notice it.

"When we get to the hospital we have to wait for security to escort us in." The officer started, breaking the silence. "We'll have to cuff you to the bed for everyone's protection. Then, I'll have to stay with you until you can be released."

"I just want to go home." I replied.

"What's the back story here?" He asked. I looked out the window and saw we were sitting at a red light. I sighed and leaned back.

"He was my boyfriend. My parents didn't quite like him, or me with him. My parents and I weren't getting along anyways..." I looked at the cars out the window as we started moving again. "Got thrown out, moved in with him, and was really, really, unhappy." I paused. "They're good people, but I want to go home. I told Sean that...and he wasn't okay with it."

"So you asked him to take you home?"

"Yeah," I replied. "He didn't want to. So, I started walking. He chased me down in the truck, and I tried to get away by jumping the fence to the parking lot. We had our words and then you guys showed up."

"Did he hit you or anything?" The officer asked, studying me in the rear-view mirror.

"No...why?"

64

"Your shirt is torn."

"Oh." I said, looking down at the large hole in my shirt. "The fence…" I started. "It got caught when I was climbing it."

We continued to drive in silence until we pulled up to the hospital. My stomach dropped as I was escorted into the building, the officer guiding me by my arm. It was the worst hospital in the state- with the highest death rate and worst reputation. I got another pat down by a security officer and the officer and I went in. The security officer followed us into the room.

"We don't have the security or staff to sit with her." The security officer told the police officer. "You can help her gown up and cuff her to the bed." The security officer looked at me as if I was a rodent, or some other filth of the earth. I pursed my lips and glared at him, fighting the urge to tell him what I thought of him, the red-faced, obese, rent-a-cop he was.

"I don't want to leave my cuffs." The officer said. "What's my other option?"

"You stay with her." Security huffed.

"Fine." The officer responded. "It's a slow night." He looked to me and gave me a small half smile. "I suppose we're going to be friends."

"I guess so." I said, shrugging my shoulders.

It was at this point that the officer finally figured out that I had slipped out of my cuffs as he went to uncuff me and my arms were in front of me instead of backwards.

He gave me a dirty look and then looked to the grotesque security officer.

"She needs to be in a gown." He said as he threw the gown on the floor at my feet. "Doctors will be in when they can." Then, with a huff, he spun around and left the room.

The officer un-cuffed me and looked at me, leaning in quietly. "I'm not going to change you." He started as the click of the cuffs released my hands. "I'm going to trust you on this one." He held up a finger. "If you do anything, and I mean anything, I will take you down to Metro after this instead of releasing you to home."

I nodded as he released the cuffs, and rubbed my wrists and studied them. I felt literally so free from the chains. The officer stepped towards the front of the room and pulled the curtain shut, leaving me to get changed. As I began to change my clothing, I noticed a mirror in the corner of the room. I turned to it and studied myself.

Mascara streaked down my face, my hair a mess and my shirt was far more torn than I thought it was. As I pulled my hair up into a messy ponytail, I realized that I did look crazy. In fact, I looked clinically insane.

I dressed quickly, taking off my dirty and torn clothing and putting on the overly starched blue gown. As I slowly pulled open the curtain I looked to the officer.

"Officer?" I asked. "May I wash my face?" I pointed to the mirror. "I don't want to look any crazier than I already do."

"Go ahead." He said stepping back into the room and watching me. I hurried and washed my face with cold water and hospital-grade hand soap. I looked back to myself in the mirror as I finished, wiping my face with a paper towel. "Hands." The officer said. I nodded and held them out for him to re-cuff me. "Sorry, he muttered. "Until a doctor releases you I have to keep you cuffed to keep everyone safe."

"I get it." I said sadly as I sat down on the bed. We sat in silence for a few moments, me looking around the room. An empty silver tray, a locked computer station, the ugliness of the beige walls, it all made me feel nauseated. Lying back on the bed, I immediately felt exhausted.

It had been weeks since I had actually rested. Weeks of working non-stop, working two jobs, running errands, not sleeping at night, stress... it started to take a toll on my mind and on my body. I blinked, trying to stay awake.

"Why don't you turn on the TV since you're stuck here?" I asked the officer, lifting my hands to point to the wall remote. He nodded and flipped the television on, sitting back in the recliner. We watched Animal Planet in silence for about thirty minutes before a nurse rushed into the room.

"You need to pee in this cup." He said, slamming a plastic cup down on the silver tray and leaving the room.

"I think you're going to need to help me find a

potty. And uncuff me. I don't think I can pee in a cup cuffed." I said, feeling sheepish.

"They do it all the time in jail...and prison." He replied, standing up and stretching.

"Seriously?" I asked. He nodded and chuckled as we walked out into the busy hallway of the emergency room. We dodged a gurney, ducked into a wrong hallway and received many dirty looks before finding a bathroom. Once we did, he uncuffed one hand, cuffing the other to the handicap rail and allowed me to pee alone.

Awkwardly, I tried to pee in the cup. I was eighteen and had never done a urine test before, so as I tried to position the cup correctly with one hand, I pondered what they were testing for. I wondered why the emergency room nurse didn't tell me what they were testing for, but instead, I sat there awkwardly.

The whole night was going that way.

I filled the cup to the brim, sealed it tightly, wrapped it in a paper towel, and handed it to the officer as he re-cuffed me. As we walked back to my room, a nurse took it from us, "I'll run it!" She yelled as she hurried off.

Another hour passed before anyone walked into my room. At this point I was annoyed. Annoyed with the handcuffs. Annoyed with the doctors and nurses and how no one was communicating with me. Annoyed with my boyfriend, or ex-boyfriends. Annoyed with my life. As the older man walked into my room, I sighed loudly as he looked to his clipboard.

"Ms. Rodriguez." He started.

"No." I interrupted.

"You're pregnant." He continued, ignoring me. "I'll send OBGYN down immediately."

"Two problems." I said in response, quickly sitting up. "One, I'm not Ms. Rodriguez. Two, I'm a virgin, and you can bet your ass I ain't the virgin Mary, so there is no way in hell I am pregnant." I snapped.

"Doctor, I have her driver's license right here, I can show you that this is Ms. Donner, not Ms. Rodriguez." The Officer said, sitting up and pointing to the clipboard full of all of his paperwork.

"Shit." The doctor replied, walking back to the nurses station and then returning to my room moments later with a different clipboard. "Uh," He started. "You have a UTI." He responded dully.

"Can I be uncuffed now?" I asked.

"Wait. Why are you cuffed?" The doctor responded.

"Psych." The officer said. "We were called for an SI."

"Are you actively trying to kill yourself?" The doctor asked. It was as if a truly awful actor was reading a poorly written script and I wanted to burst out laughing. Instead, I bit my lip and shook my head. "She can be uncuffed." He announced. "You can go." He told the officer.

The officer un-cuffed me, then handed me my

driver's license and my other belongings. "Behave yourself." He said, pointing to me as he started to leave.

I felt sad to see him go. It was like having an unspoken friend there to protect you, and after the faux pregnancy announcement I felt like I needed the friend. As he left me alone with the doctor, I felt truly alone.

"Ms. Donner, I'm going to prescribe you some medications for the UTI." He read off of the clipboard. I nodded and leaned back into the bed, pulling my knees up to my chest. "You will not be eligible to leave until a psych doctor clears you."

Without another word the doctor left, and it left me alone in this emergency room. I had the pathetically thin gown and the worn television remote. I sighed and found a sheet in a drawer from a table in the corner of the room and pulled it up and around myself and laid my bed into a flat position. I sighed and laid down, trying to get some rest. Within seconds my eyes fluttered shut, and with my last conscious moment I prayed that this was all a bad dream and that I would wake up someplace far away from all of this.

"Ms. Donner?" A soft voice coaxed. "Ms. Donner...I'm the psych doctor. They asked me to come talk to you to see about going home."

Groggily, I sat up quickly, rubbing my eyes. "Yeah, sorry." I grumbled. "It's, uh… It's been a long few weeks."

"It's quite alright." He said. "Let me give you a cup of water." He suggested, stepping out of the room. I forced my eyes to open and looked around. Not a thing had changed, and I still couldn't tell what time it was. "Here." He said, returning to my room with a cup of cool water.

I nodded as he handed it to me and thankfully, drank all of it. It was the first thing I had to drink it hours, only allowing me to realize how awful I felt. It was a refreshing feeling though, feeling something other than numb.

"Thank you." I said quietly, nodding to him. He smiled and crossed one leg over the other, balancing his metal clipboard on his lap. He was dressed awfully well, perfectly pressed tan slacks, a baby blue button up and a dark blue tie that was pinned to his shirt with a large golden tie clip.

"So let's talk." He started, smiling at me.

"Okay, let's talk." I agreed.

"According to our records and the police records you were having an awfully rough night." He started. "The officers paperwork said that you and your boyfriend got into a fight, you tried to leave and he refused to let you, and in the process you became suicidal." He flipped through his paperwork on his clipboard. "The officer noted your clothing was torn and you looked distressed."

"A meltdown of biblical proportions." I said. "Wild hair and wrent clothing." I replied dryly.

"They said that the boyfriend, or ex boyfriend?" He paused. "He called the police and here you are, does that sound correct?"

"Basically." I replied. "I need to be really, really honest." I started, leaning forward. "This, this is crap. All of this is crap."

"It does not sound like my usual psych situation for an emergency room patient." He replied, "But since we're here, let's do the assessment. If you're good, you're great. If you're not, we'll get you some help. Either way, you'll get out of here tonight and get on the road to healing."

"Fair enough." I mumbled.

"Have you ever thought of suicide before tonight?" He started. "Have you ever thought about ways to harm yourself?" He started.

"Haven't we all?" I asked in response. "I mean, seriously, even if it's meant in jest, hasn't everyone contemplated if they were to off themselves how they'd do it?" I looked at him as he pursed his lips, studying my face. "I'm not going to pass, am I?" I asked.

"I've just never been given that answer." He replied. "It's an interesting response."

"Sorry," I said, leaning back into the bed and covering myself with the sheet.

The questions were full of ways that I'd contemplated suicide, what stresses me out, and what happens when I'm stressed. I tried to answer them honestly, but I felt like I was butchering the answers and made a bigger mess of my life by even talking to this man.

"Ms. Donner, let's get you some antidepressants." He started. "Most people only take them for a few months, so you'll be off of them before you know it. Also, I'm going to get you something to help you sleep." He added. "It seems as if that may be the biggest of the problems you have."

As I got back into my clothes and got my prescriptions in my hands I headed out to the parking lot. It was still pitch black outside, but as I looked up to the sky I noticed how far the moon had traveled. The parking lot was empty and as I began to walk through it I heard a whistle and saw Sean climb out of a car. I felt my stomach drop as he started towards me, wrapping an arm around me.

"Hey, let's get you home." He said. "I nodded. He looked at my bag with medications in it and my drivers license. "Are those your meds?" He asked. I nodded, feeling sad. "I've got some water in the car, you can take them now."

Before I could buckle myself in the car he was handing me the water and encouraging me to take them. I looked to him, then took my medications. Before we got to the main roads to head home, I was asleep.

The next morning I awoke in a guest bedroom at Sean's parents house. I felt ill as I laid there, staring at the ceiling and the light seeping in through the curtains. It was as if I couldn't move, my body weighed three times the amount it should, and as I laid there, even breathing was difficult. I laid there for what felt like hours, not moving, barely breathing.

Sean opened the door and looked into the room. "Hey." He whispered. "How are you?" He asked, sitting down on the bed next to me.

"Sean." I started to whisper in response. "Please, take me home. To my real home."

Sean was obviously upset but he helped me pack my things. My medications had me so sedated that I could barely move, so during the entire process I was like a narcoleptic and continued to fall asleep in the middle of any progress I had been making. By sunset that evening, I was loaded up in the truck and heading home.

When we got there my dad and my brother helped nearly carry me into the house and into my bed. It was stripped down to a single pillow and a fresh sheet, and as I laid down, groggy and listless, my brother placed a blanket over me, tucking me in. Meanwhile, my dad took my things out of Sean's truck and came upstairs to check on me.

"What the hell is wrong with you?" He asked, entering my room and causing me to jump awake.

"They gave me all of these medications." I mumbled. "And they made me take them late last night. And I'm still this way." My dad started digging through my duffel bags and finally found the medications. He read

74

each bottle and set them on my dresser.

"They'll take some time to get used to." He finally said. Then patted my back. "Get some sleep… I'll tell mom your home."

Weeks had passed and I was back to work. College had started and I was starting to get back up on my feet. I had purchased a truck from my uncle, my aunt's old truck and I spent my free time fixing it up. Sean and I hadn't spoken much since the day he took me back to my parents home. He was upset with me, and I wasn't sure that I wouldn't' be upset if I were in his shoes. We had agreed to meet one evening in an elementary school parking lot.

"Dani, you went crazy."

"I know, Sean." I reply dryly.

"What are you wanting from this?" He asked, leaning over and looking at me.

"I don't know." I replied. "I just wanted to talk to you." I looked back to him. He looked annoyed and in his annoyance he threw his glass soda bottle down on the ground in front of my truck. I sighed and looked back up to the sky, feeling defeated.

"What do you want?" He demanded.

"Clear answers?" I asked. "Like...are we together or not?" He started at me, studying me. He looked me up and down and then sighed, leaning back on the windshield next to me.

"What do you want me to say?" He asked, his

hazel eyes staring me down.

"I don't know." I said. "I just want to heal, I want to go on with my life and I need to know if you're with me or not."

He leaned forward, jumping off of my truck. As he started to walk away, I felt sad and started to feel my eyes welling up with tears. I sat up to see him pause and look back, and as he did so he waved and then got into his truck and left.

I started to sob, and as the tears fell down my cheeks and my chest got tight, I recalled that I had rescue meds in my pocket. I slipped a tablet under my tongue, then pulled out my cell phone to call my day to come and rescue me, knowing I couldn't drive while on it.

Blinking, I looked at myself in the mirror, sighing and running my fingers through my messy hair. I dropped my head against the wall and looked up to the ceiling, watching the clouds roll part the small part of the window that I could peek out of. Moving felt like it was going to take so much effort, so in an attempt to save energy, I simply didn't move. My pulse could be heard pounding loudly in my ears. I turned my head and started at my door as the doorknob rattled. It twisted and my mother entered the room, peeking her head in slowly.

"You're up." She said in a monotone voice. I nodded slowly. "You gotten out of bed yet?"

"No I whispered." My voice raspy and my throat

dry. "I need to pee." I whispered.

"Well, go pee." She said. "If you want to come downstairs I can make you something to eat." I nodded and then hung my feet over the edge of the bed. I started down at my feet, watching them as they dangled there.

Stepping onto them, I felt numb and weak. I walked, carefully, stumbling every few steps as I headed towards the bathroom. As I got there, I stopped and stared at myself in the mirror, grasping to the bathroom counter for support. My blue eyes were red and puffy, my body weak, and I felt hopeless as I studied myself in the mirror.

"You went crazy." I whispered to myself, brushing the hair out of my eyes and a hot tear rolling down my cheek. "You went crazy."

"The last time I was here at therapy I noticed that my therapist had a box of toys in the corner. I noticed a crown in the box, a scepter and a royal cape. For a moment, a very long moment, I seriously considered putting them on. I considered prancing around the room; declaring myself the Queen of this therapy office and knighting my therapist. I figured that if I had to be in therapy, I ought to have a damn good reason for me to be here.

Plus, red capes are kind of awesome."
Journal Entry, February 2015

"I just want to live. Not just live, but really live, be alive. I want to try new foods and eat foods that are awful for me. I want to enjoy what I eat. I want to actually taste food. I want to do and do things. I want to try things I never have before and go places I haven't been before. I want to go hiking. I want to catch a fish. I want to go to a club. I want to sit in an old man's bar. I want to enjoy my body and what I do to it. I want vibrant, colored tattoos, full of meaningful art and beautiful style. I want to wear clothes that I feel fabulous in and enjoy and shamelessly wear cotton blends. I want to write my novel. To pour myself into paper and bleed words. To create art is to create life, and I intend to create a world changing life. I want to get drunk and write, tapping into that raw emotion that I can only hit up once I am inebriated. I want to feel the burn of that truth serum as it goes down my throat, leaving me forced into exposing the beautiful and painful truth."
Journal Entry, March 2015

Sunrise High

When a child colors a picture of the ocean, they usually use an unrealistic color. Usually it is either a light blue or a dark blue, similar to the beach photos you see in overpriced travel advertisements. The brightness of the blue makes you think that the water is clear and perfect, and the darkness reminds you of a clean blue water, like the kinds you see in dolphin documentaries. As I looked up to the sky, the sun kissing my cheeks, I smiled and stared up at the sky. The sky was so unrealistically blue, as if it was colored in by a child.

I once asked a patient why they moved to Utah from the Midwest. The patient and I had grown close over the few days I had tended her and I had learned all about her life and adventures. I wondered why a person would leave their family and their home to come to a place that was so dull to me. She smiled at me.

"When I flew into Salt Lake for a layover," she started. "I looked up and saw the skies as we were about to land. They were so blue. They were like the blue skies you see in books, or in music videos. They were so blue that you could see your dreams come true."

That moment sat in the forefront of my mind and showed itself every time a day was as beautiful as the one that was encircled around me. I had been walking up a hill just outside of my work and had paused to admire the day. I stood in the middle of a parking lot and simply admired the cloudless day and the deep blue of the sky above me. Inhaling, I paused and smiled.

It had been so long since I had felt this well. Many long nights had come before this day. Many nights where hot tears hitting a cold pillow took my ability to sleep from me. Longer days were depression had taken away all my energy and will to live. Afternoons that could have been spent with my young son had been spent under the covers in my dark room, trying to collect my thoughts and regain any sanity to make it through a few hours of my life. Since the last time I had felt this well I had tried to end my life, and more importantly, tried to save it. Now that I was back to feeling this way I was embracing it like I never had before.

My body felt as if it was buzzing. Perhaps it was, but I was too energized to feel it. It felt as if I had had too many energy drinks and was on a caffeine overload. My fingers itched to do something as they hung at my sides, my index and middle fingers rubbed the seam of my pants, twitching to do something. My feet began to move again and I continued up the steep hill, continuing my walk back up to the top of the foothills.

One of my first bouts of mania occurred when I was only seventeen years old. I was young, dumb and reckless as it was, but then my mental illness kicked in and allowed me to up the ante already set by my peers. As I looked around me and admired the view of Salt Lake City, I was reminded of that first bout of mania, the first time I felt this buzzing and the feeling of life.

It was just before sunrise, in late May. For the last nine months my best friend and I had raced each other to school in order to secure our favorite parking spots. The battle between the parking spot I was rolling my little old car into was ferocious, and included my friend spray painting his name into the parking stall. Usually on mornings like these when I beat him to the parking stall, he'd park on the grass next to it and block me in or park so close to my car with his truck that I couldn't back out. Of course, that didn't stop him or my other friends from physically picking up my car and moving it to the other end of the parking lot, or even towing it onto the baseball fields.

Stupidity like the one surrounding the parking stall aside, we were meeting just before sunrise for academic purposes. While we all took part in outrageously stupid antics, we actually were all very smart and had perfect grade point averages. This morning, my best friend Dale and I were meeting to study for our English finals.

Placing my little Volkswagen in park, I did a thorough once-over on my car. I checked to make sure I had all of my belongings that I needed for the day's activities and that I had locked all of my doors. I stepped out of the car and locked it up, ensuring that it was secured so that my friends had to work to play any pranks on me. Once I was sure it was safe and secure, I headed towards the gray industrial building they called a school.

Before I could get to the double doors to head inside, I heard the roar of my friend Dale's truck. A few months back, he hit a pothole and his already rusted muffler had fallen off and had gotten lost in the gutter of an already busy highway. Now, this truck roared loudly in the crisp and previously silent morning air. I chuckled to myself as I heard it and paused to wait for my friend to arrive. Within a moment he did, his old baby blue truck bouncing onto the grass next to my car and bucking forward with a quick screech of the brakes as he placed it in park. He jumped out of the truck and smiled at me.

"Listen sweetheart, you need to quit parking in my spot. It does have my name on it you know." He said, pointing to my car. I laughed loudly and shook my head.

"No way." I said, starting to walk towards him. "If I get here first, that spot is mine."

"Eh, fuck it." He said, spitting onto the sidewalk. He then leaned into his truck and pulled out a brown, wrinkled McDonald's bag from the passenger seat. "You didn't wear your fake cowboy boots did you?"

"Nope," I said as I looked to my feet. The summer before I saved up all summer to buy a pair of high-heeled cowboy boots. They were comfortable and the closest I was going to get to wearing high heels like my classmates did. I loved those boots more than anything, but my friends all thought it was silly to wear three inch heeled cowboy boots when a normal boot with an inch heel would do the job just fine. Today I had too much to do and didn't want to compromise my own comfort, so I had donned my worn-out and dirty white sneakers. "Why?"

"Because we're having breakfast." He said with a grin.

In the months before, I had not been myself. I had been seriously depressed and suffered my first fit of anxiety. My parents saw it as a normal bout of being a teenager, but my friends knew something bigger was going on. My friend Dale had reached out to me and told me that he was going to push me to my own limits and do whatever he could to make me feel better. I hadn't wanted to feel better, let alone could feel better until recently. As I saw the bag of food and inhaled the aroma of the high-calorie disaster in a bag, I smiled.

"Lets." I said.

"Let's go." He said walking past me.

Without question, I followed him. He and I headed towards the wood shop at our school. Behind the shop itself, we had a large red shipping container placed, storing the students wood shop projects. Between the shipping container and the shop was a ventilation system that was fenced in. As we approached the school, Dale took a sharp turn and headed towards the shipping container. Turning to his side he slid in between the fence and the shipping container, and while pressing his back against it, took his foot into a hole in the fence and started to climb.

"Uh, where are we going to have this breakfast?" I asked as I watched my friend clamber up to the top of the fence and pull himself up and onto the shipping container.

"On the roof." He said casually. "Come on, let me help you up."

Following Dale's lead, I pressed my back into the shipping container and hooked my feet into the holes in the chain link fence. I scooted up the container and with the help of Dale got on top of it next to him. Being wildly afraid of heights, I felt my stomach churn into knots as I looked to the school below me.

"Oh boy." I whispered to myself. Dale smiled, then with a hurl, tossed the breakfast up and onto the roof of the school.

"Now we have to make it up there for breakfast." He said looking to me.

We stepped onto the fence dividing the shipping container with the ventilation system, then onto the ventilation system itself. It reminded me of the outside of a fast food play place, and as we climbed up and over the vents and fans, I was reminded of being a child and climbing over the slides and tunnels. As we got to the last part before the roof, a large lip that dipped down and onto the roof, I reached up to try to get there and found that I was too short. Without a word, Dale placed both hands on my hips and picked me up. With a quick oomph he lifted me over the lip and I rolled awkwardly onto the roof. The roof had gravel on it and I slid on it as I started to get to my feet, I looked to see Dale climbing up behind me.

We got to our feet and looked to the east. While Dale began to get our breakfast back, I stared at the sunrise. It was brilliant, shades of pink, orange, red and yellow filling the sky and reflecting off of the clouds. It was like something that you only see painted or on postcards. From as high up as we were, we were able to see the city as well, the sun reflecting off of the buildings and creating brilliant reflections of an already brilliant sunrise.

"Holy shit." I whispered.

"Lets sit down and eat." Dale said, approaching me and grabbing my wrist.

We walked further away from the edge of the roof and towards a ventilation box. We sat down and Dale pulled out some cheap burritos and a couple of energy drinks, setting it up like a picnic on the roof. As I sat down next to my friend, I inhaled slowly, trying to take in everything I was feeling.

I realized I felt like I was buzzing, that I felt like the lights inside of the school that I was sitting on top of. It felt like I was living those pictures, like the ones commonly used as advertisements for perfume in magazines. I could almost smell the fragrance now, the vague smell of the last flowers of spring lingering in the air. Looking to my friend, I could only smile.

"I feel like I'm alive." I said.

"Dumb ass, you are alive." He replied with a laugh.

It was as if suddenly I wanted to do so much, and be so much. As I took a bite into the cheap and poorly made burrito I had a yearning to eat amazing foods, and each bite of the food I was eating tasted much better than it should have.

I thought of all of the things my friends had been doing to live and I suddenly wanted to do them. I wanted to have sex. I wanted to skip classes to go try new foods. I wanted to stay out past curfew. I wanted to smoke marijuana, or peyote like my friends commonly did. I wanted to lie out in the middle of nowhere and drink beer while the radio played loud from our trucks. All these things I'd never had a desire to do, I suddenly was craving, nearly salivating from the want to do these things.

"Whooo!" I suddenly yelled, standing up and throwing my food wrapper off the edge of the building. "I feel so alive!"

Dale laughed and stood up with me, smiling at me as I began dancing wildly in the silence of the morning. It was as if I couldn't control myself and I had no control over my own body or mind. Instead of fighting it, I just went with it, allowing myself to do whatever I wanted to do.

"Dance with me." I said, grabbing his hands. Without any hesitation Dale and I danced on the roof. Arms waved in the morning air, asses shook to the sound of silence. At one point I even turned around and danced as if I was in a club, grinding up on my friend awkwardly. Finally, we turned to each other and embraced each other, holding each other in silence. While my soul felt like it was trembling inside of my body, I felt the best and most euphoric I had ever felt into my life. It was perfect.

"Hey!" A voice yelled loudly. Startled, we both jumped and peeked over the end of the building to see one of the schools police officers yelling up to us. "Get down from there!" He yelled, waving his arm in one hand and the hand radio in the other.

"Oh shit." I said, looking to Dale.

"This is where we run." He replied.

As I approached my work building, nearing the end of my lunch break walk, I found myself looking at the roof of the building. The same buzzing and trembling feeling filled my soul and I felt the exact same as I did all those years ago. It was as if I felt like my old self, whoever that self was. I stopped as I reached the parking lot and studied the building, the bright blue skies behind it.

"What are you looking at?" A coworker asked as

they passed me.

      "Just wondering if I could climb up onto that roof." I replied with a sly smile.

What I Still Don't Know

If I were to tell anyone starting treatment of Bipolar anything; it would be to be strong, to stay optimistic, and to accept that you just don't know. The first two bits of advice are very self explanatory; keep your chin up and don't get pissed off when you need to change meds or when they react poorly. Easy peasy. The last one is the difficult one - the one that will become a phrase deeply embedded into your daily routine. "I don't know," you'll say. And you won't just say it - you'll know it.

People will ask questions. They won't understand, so they'll ask why you purchased a year's worth of cleaning supplies during a high phase - and you won't know. They'll ask why you didn't attend their party during a low phase - and you won't know. It doesn't matter if they're asking your favorite color or what you want for dinner, the answer is always the same. "I don't know."

There is enough about life that I never understood as it was. I could never understand how the stock market worked, and I surely wasn't about to comprehend nuclear fusion. The pharmacological workings of medications in the human body always fascinated me - but I didn't understand it one bit. No matter how much I loved watching reruns of 'How it's Made,' Most of the time I still never understood how they made it. Life itself was already a big enough mystery to me, and realizing that my new diagnosis was going to make that more difficult really weighed on me.

Some nights are still difficult to comprehend all of this; realizing that I just do not know.

I don't know if I will be the same person in the morning that I am right now. That makes it impossible to plan things with my family.

I don't know why I'll be doing whatever it is I'll be doing with my next high phase. It's so difficult to explain to others that the literal urge to clean keeps me awake at night and I physically cannot sleep until that bathroom is spotless.

I don't know when my next low will hit. I don't know what will trigger it. It could be anything from a sad movie on television to simply having period cramps. I don't know why my body feels like it weighs double what I normally do when I'm low. And I don't know how to fight it.

Simply put; I don't know.

It was my second visit in my psychiatrist's office when I first realized this. She had written a diagnosis on top of a post-it note and then left the room, leaving me alone to be with my thoughts and her notes on the desk. I clasped my hands tightly around each other and fiddled with my wedding band nervously. I signed and peered over towards the desk so I could see her note better. "Bipolar - I vs II ?"

It didn't matter what level I was, it was all the same to me. I was a Bipolar patient.

Slowly sinking back into her purple couch I let my body go numb and allowed my racing mind to take over. I wondered what the official diagnosis meant for my life, what life would look like now. Obviously it meant medications and therapy - but I pondered what implications all of it would have on my life.

What medications would I be on? Who would I be on my medications? What would I be like? What things about me - or my life - would change?

My psychiatrist returned to her office and shut the door firmly behind her. She smiled at me as she walked towards her desk and sat back down in her large black leather chair. As she sat, she faced me, her knees now touching mine. "You ready to get started on some treatment?" She asked optimistically.

"I don't know." I whispered quietly.

During the treatment of any mental illness, you're set to see a handful of providers over many appointments for the next few years. In my time seeking treatment I've spent what is close to a hundred hours in therapy. Between my psychiatrist, my therapist and my EAP counselor. I'm used to large couches with big pillows, hot offices with leather chairs, and providers with clicky pens and tassels on their shoes.

After my official diagnosis, I was assigned to a new counselor at a new therapy practice. He wore jeans and sneakers, he used pens that didn't click and spoke to me more honestly than any other counselor I had before.

The thing he did that really bothered me what what we came to call 'check in's.' Basically, a check in occurs at the beginning of each appointment. He would ask three seemingly simple questions before we could discuss anything else and use that to gauge where I was. While it is a great concept and obviously derived from solid therapeutic foundations, these check in's annoyed the hell out of me.

"It's time for a check in." He'd say cheerily as he prepared a fresh sheet of paper from his notebook. "How are you doing physically?"

The first question was always the easiest question. All you had to do was make sure you were feeling something, anything. I'm pretty sure he was just making sure I had a pulse before we got started by asking this question. I'd always reply with something like 'energized, or 'drained.'

"Okay," he'd reply as he'd scribble notes on whatever I had just said onto his notepad. "And emotionally?" He'd ask, crossing one leg up over the other. "How are you feeling emotionally?"

This one was trickier to answer, but I was convinced that any answer I gave was a safe one, even if it from a bad place. The answers to this one never really changed if I am to be totally honest. I was a bipolar patient, the product of a dysfunctional domestic upbringing.

"I'm fried." I'd answer, because it was the closest I could answer to what I was feeling. I did feel fried - like a light that had just burnt out; the filament still trying to glow inside the fractured bulb but obviously never going to work.

"Okay." He'd say as he scribbled the last of his notes towards the far edge of his paper. I'd watch him and with dread wait for the last and the worst of the questions. "Spiritually." He'd continue. "How are you feeling spiritually?" He'd ask.

There was always a pause at this point, or a simple sigh as I looked past my therapist to the wall. I never really knew what I wanted to say in response to that question. I don't know if I even knew what he was asking. The Merriam-Webster Dictionary defines spirituality as *the quality or state of being concerned with religion or religious matters.*

"I, uh…" I'd begin quietly. I felt embarrassed. I wasn't sure what he wanted me to say. I wasn't sure if I cared. I wasn't even sure if I was supposed to care about it. "I don't know." I'd say quietly.

After months of these check ins I finally groaned loudly in frustration and hung my head as he asked me that damned question again. "Look." I started with a deep sigh, putting my face into my hands. "I don't know." I confessed. "I don't know if I'm ever going to know."

My therapist set his notepad on the couch next to him and leaned forward towards me. "It's okay." He said calmly, smiling. "It's okay not to know." I shook my head and looked to the ceiling, I was fighting back tears. "Knowing you don't know is more than half of this battle."

I had actively been seeking treatment for my Bipolar Disorder for about seven months when I decided to 'announce' my diagnosis to my friends and family through the social media platform, Facebook. I'm sure it was a manic phase that prompted me to type up the confession to my loved ones, and before I knew it my phone was buzzing nonstop. Each time I checked it I found something different; words of encouragement from friends, negative comments from family, accusations from acquaintances. It was all out there, and so was their replies.

Within the fast paced flurry of digital activity this

confessional turned into a 'ask the crazy person anything' style threat before I knew it and questions were pouring in quicker than I could answer them.

My phone buzzed in the palm of my hand and I turned the screen on so that I could see the question on there. It felt as if I had eaten a brick for breakfast. My stomach dropped into my abdomen and I found myself moving slowly from a standing position to a sitting position on the floor next to my bed. My world was placed on pause as I read the question.

"I am so glad you are seeking treatment." It started. "When will you be back to normal?"

Normal is something that doesn't exist. We're all taught that in school and now in our families and in our culture. Normal isn't something to strive for, or to be proud of. But in this moment, I wanted normality so badly. I looked up from my phone and tried to recall from my memories a time I ever felt normal, or perhaps even acted normal. In the midst of trying to rationalize this friends question, I realized that I will never have the luxury of ever really knowing anything again.

These friends will never have to question when the next bout of depression will cause suicidal tendencies and keep them out of work for days. They'll never have to wonder if they'll lose enough control to cut themselves again. They'll never have to wonder what will be left of them when this bout passes. They won't have the struggle of not knowing themselves enough to know what they will or won't do when they get low.

These friends will never have to question if they're going to be sleeping that week or not due to a high phase. They won't have to question what the literal buzzing inside of their head will drive them to do. They won't have to wonder what they will try to do to themselves in a high place. These friends won't have to ask the questions that I do; and they won't have to know the answer.

I knew the answer; I also knew that I didn't have the heart to write the answer. Instead, I responded with an all too familiar answer, "I don't know."

The truth is, I am never going to know anymore. And as a bipolar patient that is something that I have to adapt and accept.

I don't know if I am going to like mint ice cream tomorrow or raspberry ice cream. That is something that literally changes with my mood swings - and who knows who I will be by then. I don't know if I am going to listen to Top 40 Radio tomorrow or listen to an NPR podcast - something that also identifies with my swings. I have no idea if I am going to have energy and work my ass off tomorrow or if I am going to have to call in sick to work because I wake up drained and suicidal.

I don't know if I'm still going to be 'me' when this is all said and done. I don't know if this is forever thing, or a just for now thing. The only thing I do know is that I am going to continue to have a hell of time trying to figure it out.

"I have done so many strange things since starting my mental health journey. I've written. I've cut my own flesh. I've sang loudly in the car, and I've drank the sting of the pain until I was blacked out. I've scrubbed things clean and slowly died under a pile of garbage. I've tried to die and failed, and I've tried to live and have yet to flourish."
Journal Entry, April 2015

"The attempts to focus today have been interesting. I keep telling myself, "Okay Dani, focus. Think." And it isn't working. What is working, ever so slightly, is narrating my life, but then I lose focus as I try to add juice to the simple story. "Dani is charting on a patient" turns into, "the blonde heroine sits slumped at the computer, her hand weak from the imminent carpal tunnel syndrome and her eyes raw and tired. As she repetitively clicks buttons on the screen she sighs." Then I'm back to the beginning. "FOCUS DANI. THINK."
Journal Entry, February 2015

"I am a diamond. Not just because it is my birthstone, but because of who I am. I can look so transparent, so bland, but I can also sparkle and shine. My situation, my childhood turned me from coal (while ugly, still useful, but far from rare), and the stress and pressure of life will change me at a molecular, cellular level. I'm going to become a diamond, but the bigger struggle is remembering that."
Journal Entry

Dear Family

To my dearest family and friends,

If you are reading this, congratulations, you have officially outlived me. I'd like to award you with a plaque, or even a pat on the back, but alas, all you get is these smart-assed musings of a fiery young woman. I apologize I couldn't offer you something better; like money, or antiques or even tales of travel and adventures. I will admit that I lived a dull and boring life, but I did find ways to fill it with zest and pulse-racing moments... usually due to my big mouth and larger than life personality. If you are reading this, my dearest family and friends, I'd like to offer you some instructions; Dear Family, please do this and not that.

Dear Family, in lieu of flowers, I want you to set up a donation for English and Literature classes, donations to libraries, anything to protect the literary arts. We have a serious issue with spelling and literature in this day and age and I want to do my part to contribute to the rescue and conservation efforts. Throw a vintage hardcover book from the Salvation Army on my casket and call it my wreath. If you have to set it up in my name to make it happen, so be it, but whatever you do, please don't stand by idly and watch the world get more and more illiterate.

Dear Family, please mention my good aspects at my funeral. You are all very apt to point out my bad or unfavorable aspects since I am alive, but now that I am gone, please take the good and elaborate on those. Let them grow and flourish like flowers blooming in the spring. See what I did there? That poetic beauty? Yeah, please focus on that kind of stuff.

Dear Family, if I am dead or missing please take my best Facebook photo to give to the media. I know I have sent you many selfies over the years that you'll be tempted to share, but please, let's keep the crossed eyes, silly faces and tongue sticking out photos between us. I'd like to world to believe I was a five foot eight and one hundred twenty pound supermodel with great breasts. Don't let me down on this one guys, I'm counting on you to do at least this one.

Dear Family, please take care of each other. Enough with the neurotic tendencies and the holidays so dysfunctional that even the psychologists don't want to be around us. While it was fun, it mostly gave us memories and something for me to write about. Since I'm gone, we can quit with the crazy and focus on the fantastic. Create memories, holidays and traditions. Cultivate a relationship with each other that is unbreakable. If you cannot do anything more, at least decide to have each others' backs. I was always fiercely loyal in life, carry this on in the wake of my death.

Dear Family, I am going to give my husband the password for my Facebook page. Brother, you and he are going to be in charge of posting on it every so often to freak my friends out. Post comments on current events, or comment on things I'd have an opinion on. Please make sure to write it as if I was writing it from the afterlife. Please don't forget to drop a few curse words in there to keep it legitimate. If one person sends a private message making sure I am really deceased, this has been a worthwhile cause.

Dear Family, if I die doing something stupid, please be the first to say so. Nothing would make me happier in those circumstances to have a viewing talk like when our family friend died. His grandmother stood up and started her talk with the words "you little shit." If I die doing something stupid, reckless, or wild, by all means make fun of me for it. Nothing would make me feel better than hearing a talk from the afterlife by my brother, who is chewing me out and calling me an idiot for swinging on an oiled up pole just outside the bus stop. Nothing would be more real to my life than my dad giving a eulogy where he chews me out for running my mouth in the ghetto and getting shot.

Dear Family, if I find out you raise hell of any kind that is unwarranted, I *will* haunt you. I will also go so far as to make ghost friends who will haunt you as well. If you pull any of the shit that some of these families pull when their loved ones die (marches, protests, attacks), you will have an entire ghost gang haunting you day in and day out. In honor of me, my somewhat good name, and for all of your sakes; play quietly, play by the rules and play nice with others. Do good things and be a family that no one can say nasty things about.

Dear Family, if you create an ugly world because of my death I will ask God to send a meteor to wipe you all out. The world is ugly enough place with all the hatred, the bad attitudes and the problems within it, that it does not need you creating any more ugliness. Do not fuck with God and meteors - you saw what he did with the Dinosaurs.

Dear Family, remember all those things you told me not to do but I did anyways? Don't do some of those. And the others? Do them. Do them so much, so hard, and so often that you'll cry from breaking your own advice. But do you even know what that is? That is living. I want you to live hard, live fast, live furiously. I want you to live, clinging to life until your fingers are calloused and your knuckles are white. Live until your heart hurts, breathe and fill your lungs with the freshness of new places. Fill your mind with knowledge, capture gorgeous pictures of places with your eyes, and fill your ears with new music. And if life isn't beautiful at that moment, it is okay. Remember, you have to bleed before you can start to heal, and all of us are just walking cicatrixes.

Dear Family, I love you. And don't any of you forget it. If you do, I'll haunt you. Or send a meteor, either way, really.

With all the love that I possess; your smart-assed, fiery, wild and fantastic daughter, wife, sister, mother, and unfortunate relative,

Dani

Resources

It is estimated that over 3 million cases of Bipolar Disorder in the United States alone. This is an extremely common diagnosis, and because of how common it is, there are so many options available for those diagnosed and their loved ones. Below is a list of resources for those that have this or know someone who does.

I highly recommend that if you or someone you know needs any help that you look into these websites and locations. There is absolutely no shame in seeking help. Seeking help saved my marriage, my family, and most importantly, my life. If you or someone you know is struggling, please seek help.

Depression and Bipolar Support Alliance:
http://www.dbsalliance.org/
International Bipolar Foundation: http://ibpf.org/about-bipolar-disorder
Mental Health.Gov
https://www.mentalhealth.gov/

National Suicide Prevention Lifeline–1- 800- 273- 8255
Treatment Referral Helpline –1- 877- 726- 4727
Emergency Medical Services - 911

Acknowledgments

To my therapist, Jason, and my psychiatrist, Ann; thank you for the extensive hours of service you put into not only helping me cope with my wild mind, but helping me to see the beauty in my diagnosis. I owe it all of my wellness, and this book to you.

To my family and friends who have always been there to lend a hand, an ear or a hug. Thank you. Your simple acts of kindness have been paramount in my treatment.

To my coworkers and employer, who was so kind and understanding when I stepped up and spoke up about my mental illness. Thank you. Your flexibility and your understanding of mental illness has not only kept me sane, but safe.

And to my husband, my son, and my mother. Thank you. I wouldn't be the person I am today without your many hours of listening to my manic rambles, drying my depressive tears, and our beautiful, deep, belly laughs. You saved my life. And I owe you for it.
I love you.

Danielle Workman is a writer based out of Salt Lake City, Utah. She has a well-rounded writing portfolio, from publishing poetry at a young age, to opinion columns in her high school newspapers, but found her love of writing and her niche through blogging and essays. Aside from her more serious literature, she writes a lifestyle and family blog, This Workman Life.

Danielle lives with her husband, son, and rambunctious Rottweiler. As a family, they enjoy marathoning television shows, watching outrageous amounts of soccer and trying out drink combinations from Sonic. Danielle enjoys participating in crafting classes, couponing, and finds herself in the garden more than she'd like to admit.

Aside from writing, Danielle works in Health care, a passion and career she's had for over ten years now. Her education and training in Health Care services includes (but is not limited to) Orthopaedics, Emergency Medicine and Trauma.

Danielle would like to extend a big thank you to all of her family, friends and even the strangers that encouraged her to write this book.